Grace Hopper

The Woman Behind Computer Programming

by Nancy Loewen

PEBBLE
a capstone imprint

Little Explorer is published by Pebble,
1710 Roe Crest Drive, North Mankato, Minnesota 56003
www.capstonepub.com

Library of Congress Cataloging-in-Publication Data is available on the Library of Congress website.
ISBN 978-1-9771-0970-5 (library binding)
ISBN 978-1-9771-1057-2 (paperback)
ISBN 978-1-9771-0980-4 (eBook PDF)

Summary: Computers touch our lives every day, in countless ways, but how do they know what to do?
How do we communicate with them and they with each other? Language! Grace Hopper was a pioneer in
computer programming, a woman whose scientific research led to computer-language tools and technology
still in use today. Her story is filled with trial and error, and readers can follow the journey step by step.

Editorial Credits

Jill Kalz, editor; Kayla Rossow, designer; Svetlana Zhurkin, media researcher;
Tori Abraham, production specialist

Our very special thanks to Emma Grahn, Spark!Lab Manager, Lemelson Center for the Study of Invention
and Innovation, National Museum of American History. Capstone would also like to thank Kealy Gordon,
Product Development Manager, and the following at Smithsonian Enterprises: Ellen Nanney, Licensing
Manager; Brigid Ferraro, Vice President, Education and Consumer Products; and Carol LeBlanc, Senior Vice
President, Education and Consumer Products.

TABLE OF CONTENTS

INTRODUCTION

Have you ever played games on a smartphone? Looked up something on a computer? Watched a movie on a tablet? Then you can thank Grace Hopper!

Hopper was a pioneer in computer programming. Smart and curious, she never stopped looking for a problem to solve. Her amazing inventions still touch people around the world every day.

All of today's computer devices are tied to Hopper's work.

The Grace Hopper Celebration of Women in Computing is held every year. It's the world's largest gathering of women who work in technology.

Grace Hopper spent 43 years in the Navy, retiring as a rear admiral.

In 2016 Hopper posthumously received the Presidential Medal of Freedom from U.S. President Barack Obama. The medal is the highest civilian honor given in the United States.

OFF TO A GOOD START

Grace was born in 1906 to Walter and Mary Murray in New York City. She was a curious child. At age 7 she took apart the family's clocks. She wanted to see how they worked.

Grace married Vincent Hopper, an English professor, in 1930. They divorced in 1945.

At the time many people believed that education was more important for boys than girls. Grace's parents didn't agree. They sent their daughter to good schools. They told her to study hard. She earned degrees in mathematics and physics at Vassar College. Then she went to Yale University. There she earned a PhD in math at the age of 28.

Grace studied, slept, and ate in Vassar's Main Building.

Grace was the 11th woman to get a PhD in math from Yale. The first woman received hers in 1895.

A TERRIFIC TEACHER

Grace Hopper was more than a good student. She was a terrific teacher too. After earning her PhD, she went back to Vassar College to teach math. She taught there for more than 10 years.

It wasn't unusual for wealthy women to go to college during Hopper's time. It *was* unusual for married women to teach.

Vassar was one of the top women's colleges in the United States from 1861 to 1969.

Albert Einstein used math to explain his ideas about matter and energy.

Hopper liked to teach scientist Albert Einstein's "new and exciting" work in her classes.

At Vassar teachers could go to any class for free. Hopper sat in on lots of classes. She brought her ideas to her students. She wanted to inspire them. She saw math as a link across all areas of study.

TURNING POINT

World War II (1939–1945) changed everything for Hopper. She wanted to serve the United States. Her heart was set on joining the Navy. But at age 35, she was considered too old. She didn't weigh enough either.

The Japanese attack on Pearl Harbor, Hawaii, on December 7, 1941, pushed the United States to enter World War II.

Hopper's great-grandfather was an admiral in the Navy during the Civil War.

Hopper didn't give up. She convinced the Navy to let her in anyway. In December 1943 she joined the WAVES (Women Accepted for Volunteer Emergency Service). The program was part of the Navy Reserves. In 1944 she became a lieutenant.

Members of WAVES helped build and fix airplanes for the Navy during World War II.

Hopper graduated first in her class from the Naval Reserve Midshipmen's School at Smith College in Massachusetts in 1944.

A MATHEMATICAL ROBOT

The Navy sent Hopper to Harvard University. Her job was to work with a machine called Mark I. It was used to solve hard math problems. Mark I wasn't like today's computers. It was huge! It used paper tape with punched holes. The pattern of the holes was called code. The code told the computer what to do.

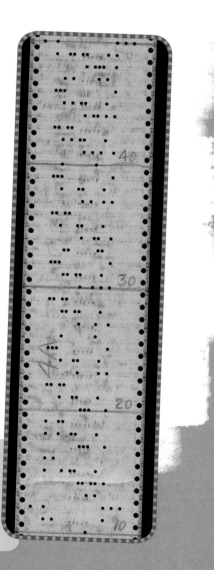

Some of the first computers got their instructions from patterns of holes punched out of rolls of paper tape.

Hopper used a keyboard to enter code onto a paper tape.

The problems Mark I solved were mostly about the war. Everything was top secret. Often Hopper didn't even know how her work was used.

THE RIGHT WOMAN FOR THE JOB

During World War II, Mark I ran 24 hours a day. Hopper put in long hours at her job. Sometimes she slept at her desk. She was the only woman in the Mark I crew. Some of the men didn't think a woman belonged there. Hopper soon changed their minds! She worked hard and had a way of bringing people together.

Later known as "Amazing Grace," Hopper pioneered the way for women in computer programming.

> Hopper wrote a 561-page manual for Mark I.

> Mark I worked almost nonstop for 16 years.

After the war Hopper stayed at Harvard. She helped design the next computers, Mark II and Mark III.

A COMPUTER BUG

Grace Hopper wasn't the first person to call a problem a "bug." But she may have been the first to apply it to computing. One day the Mark II computer quit. Hopper and her team found a dead moth inside it. Just for fun Hopper taped the moth into her log book. "The first actual case of a bug being found," she wrote. The moth is housed at the National Museum of American History.

NEW GROWTH

Only the government used the Mark computers. Some people thought they could be used by businesses too. Grace Hopper was one of those people.

The UNIVAC filled a room and weighed about 8 tons.

In the 1950s the word *UNIVAC* meant "computer" to most people. UNIVAC stood for Universal Automatic Computer.

In 1949 Hopper took a job at a computer company in Pennsylvania. The company made a computer called the UNIVAC. Like any new invention, the UNIVAC had problems. It was big. It cost a lot. And it was difficult to use.

The UNIVAC was challenged to pick who would win the 1952 U.S. presidential election. After programmers loaded the data, the room-size computer said Dwight D. Eisenhower would win. And he did.

HOPPER'S GREAT IDEA

Hopper was always trying to solve problems. She wanted better, faster ways to do things. For years she had been collecting bits of code that she used often. In 1952 she took these bits and put them on a tape. Each bit was given a call number. The computer brought up the call number. Then it could use all the code already in the system.

Hopper had invented the first compiler. It was a shortcut. And it worked!

Hopper's bosses didn't think a compiler would work. She had to work on it in her spare time.

Inside the UNIVAC lay a maze of wires, tubes, and other electronic parts.

Before Hopper's compiler all computer programs were built from scratch—even if they shared much of the same code. The process took a lot of time. Mistakes were often made.

The UNIVAC stored information on magnetic tape.

THE POWER OF WORDS

Hopper's next challenge also involved code. At the time only math experts could be programmers. They wrote code using numbers and other math symbols. Hopper thought code could be written with words. If a machine could read a symbol, why couldn't it read a letter? She thought code based on words would be more user-friendly.

Hopper kept a clock in her office that ran backward. It reminded her that most problems can be solved in many ways, not just one.

```
(14) SET OPERATION 4 TO GO TO
OPERATION 5.
(15) JUMP TO OPERATION 5.
READ-ITEM A; IF END OF DATA GO
TO OPERATION 16.
(16) TEST PRODUCT; IF EQUAL GO
TO OPERATION 18; OTHERWISE GO TO
OPERATION 17.
(17) TRANSFER A TO D. REWIND B.
```

an example of word-based code

In 1951 one UNIVAC cost more than $9 million in today's dollars (2019 estimate).

Hopper and her team made another compiler. This one used common business words. Called FLOW-MATIC the compiler helped companies pay workers, send bills, and do many other tasks.

FLOW-MATIC was in use by 1956.

A TEAM PLAYER

FLOW-MATIC was a success. But Hopper wanted to push herself even more. She wanted to create one standard language for every computer in the world.

Hopper gathered a large team of programmers. Together they created COBOL. It stood for Common Business-Oriented Language. The new language could "talk" to all computers. COBOL came out in 1959. It is still used today.

Hopper understood the importance of working as a team.

Today 80 percent of all daily business dealings around the world use COBOL.

COBOL

Report to
CONFERENCE on DATA
SYSTEMS LANGUAGES

Including
INITIAL SPECIFICATIONS
for a COMMON BUSINESS
ORIENTED LANGUAGE (COBOL)
for Programming
Electronic Digital Computers

DEPARTMENT OF DEFENSE   APRIL 1960

"If you ask me what accomplishment I'm proudest of, the answer would be all the young people I've trained over the years; that's more important than writing the first compiler."

—Grace Hopper

Hopper quickly became the face of the new language called COBOL.

GAME CHANGER

Hopper's work was quickly changing the computer world. It was also changing the business world. People began to understand that hardware and software were two different things. Lots of different programs could run on the same machines. People could more easily share what they learned. Progress could happen faster.

In 1969 Hopper was named computer science's "Man of the Year."

Grace Hopper around 1961

In the 1960s computers helped businesses print reports.

In her lifetime Hopper published more than 50 articles about computing.

"GRANDMA COBOL"

Hopper worked with computers the rest of her life. She taught classes and helped businesses solve problems. In her later years, she was a popular speaker. People liked her funny stories and sayings. They liked how she challenged them to try new ideas.

Hopper appeared on the TV news show *60 Minutes* in 1983. Three years later she appeared on *Late Night with David Letterman*.

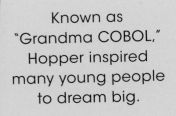

Known as "Grandma COBOL," Hopper inspired many young people to dream big.

At her public events, Hopper often handed out wires that were exactly 11.8 inches (30 centimeters) long. That was how far electricity could travel in a nanosecond (one billionth of a second).

IN THE NAVY

Grace Hopper's career in the Navy lasted for more than 40 years. She served in the Navy Reserve from 1943 until 1966, when she was forced to retire because of her age. But the next year, the Navy called her into special service to help solve computer problems. She remained in the Navy until 1986. When she finally retired for real, she was the oldest active officer and had achieved the rank of rear admiral. Her retirement celebration was held aboard the U.S.S. *Constitution,* the Navy's oldest ship.

NEVER FORGOTTEN

Grace Hopper died in 1992 at age 85. Her inventions paved the way for computer programming as we know it today. They made computers more user-friendly. Computer languages run our banks, our stores, our governments . . . even our computer games! And they all draw from the amazing work of Grace Hopper.

Hopper was buried with full military honors at Arlington National Cemetery in Virginia.

The Navy named a warship after Grace Hopper—the U.S.S. *Hopper.*

"When you have a good idea and you've tried it and you know it's going to work, go ahead and do it—because it's much easier to apologize afterwards than it is to get permission."

—Grace Hopper

One of Hopper's lasting lessons is that great ideas and teamwork can meet any challenge.

GLOSSARY

code—a system of symbols for sending messages

degree—a title given by a college when a student completes a program of study

hardware—the physical parts of a computer

inspire—to cause someone to want to do something positive

military—the armed forces that defend a country during war

Navy—the part of the U.S. military that has to do with the sea

Navy Reserve—a branch of the U.S. Navy in which people serve part-time

PhD—the highest degree a person can earn from a college or university; also called a doctorate degree; "PhD" stands for "Doctor of Philosophy"

pioneer—a person who is one of the first to try new things

posthumously—after death

programmer—a person who writes the code that tells computers what to do

software—a set of instructions that gives computers particular tasks

symbol—something that stands for something else (such as a "+" that means "add")

CRITICAL THINKING QUESTIONS

1. What were some of the ways Grace Hopper changed the world of computers?

2. Hopper thought it was important to work well with others. How do you think that affected what she was able to do?

3. From the beginning, Hopper believed that computers would be important in our daily lives. How do you think computers might be used in the future?

READ MORE

Borgert-Spaniol, Megan. *Grace Hopper: Advancing Computer Science.* STEM Superstar Women. Minneapolis: Abdo, 2018.

Pelleschi, Andrea. *Mathematician and Computer Scientist Grace Hopper.* STEM Trailblazer Bios. Minneapolis: Lerner Publications, 2017.

Wallmark, Laurie. *Grace Hopper: Queen of Computer Code.* New York: Sterling Children's Books, 2017.

INTERNET SITES

An animated video-biography of Grace Hopper
https://www.youtube.com/watch?v=Fg82iV-L8ZY

Beanz Magazine article: "Grace Hopper"
https://www.kidscodecs.com/grace-hopper/

Grace Hopper talks about nanoseconds
https://www.youtube.com/watch?v=JEpsKnWZrJ8

INDEX